THE SECRET

OF THE

STEM

Pianta

INTRODUCTION

I'm grateful for these pieces because they come from a different place and time. I hope they take you to someplace unexpected, somewhere above the clouds.

TABLE OF CONTENTS

THE SECRET OF THE STEM

Flowers long to be like the moon
emanating pink halos
in soft green-pink rings
longing for the invincibility
of the great white circle.

They find it in the base of their circle
in the secret of the stem
where lie tunnels—
the tunnels of fairies
who sing songs of joy for their small size.

IN THE PERIPHERY

We see you in the periphery. A giant lumbering, scuffing your shoes on the fairy ring of stones, each chosen carefully, each with a special secret. It's a memory of something we hold dear. You are touching each rock, and with your touch, the rocks can sing the songs they have been saving.

We have many visitors, many loved ones. They come and play their violins all night. I'm an intruder too, but I can't help but hear the singing. It comes with colors. I thought the flowers had the power, but here, the stones have their magic. They ring up in pink and green—many shades of green—and that pale color of fragrant white ginger stems.

This house has not been so full in such a long time. Come sing on the merry round! The giant has left a mark on the rocks of the cottage, and all of the ground sweepers stand still. They are afraid to move. They are afraid their tears of joy will pour down the roads and wash the giant away, but he's here, standing firm until the time when only flowers will mark where we all have been.

We blow out the candle, but from the window I still watch. The rings of color are quivering, turning into a circle glowing, into infant light, into a holy heart of sound and stone. This is the way of giants, and a giant has come to call.

IN TULLE

The feeling of tulle
reminds us of how blessed things
can be birthed.
As we walk,
the silk of tulle
blooms in the air and billows
in what feels like the width of the sky.
If in a hurry, women can grasp hoop-wide dresses
to run across a field,
but the wind finds traction
and the sound of fluttering
gives the runners pause just to hear the air
propelling itself against their will.

Bees hover
drawn to skirted flowers
but only gravity
and charity
can persuade the mighty tulle
and winged fairies
to come closer to our earthly world,
despite all our flaws,
to bestow the ways of silk.

BLUE FAN FAIRIES/SPRING IN BOSTON

A woman fails. Or is it just that the longing to see the soft curve of a shell, the imprint of a fan, a faint transparency, ceases? A dream of the blue fan fairies. They dance on the lawn in their green shoes. Their green shoes are the underside of leaves inside, and the glossy side, outside. They catch the slick of the blue transparent fans. Come visit me, I cry inside. Come see me. I remember in the summer, soft colors glowed around me, and in my chest, I'd feel so full. Let me feel that fullness. A woman fails. A heart grows cold. It disappears, not in a warm breath, but chills itself and coast the insides with frost. It dries then, and the insides are tempered. Nothing to get angry about. Inside there's no furniture to knock about.

A woman fails. A heart doesn't long for another. To long for the fairies is to long for a dream that is safe. A big, harmless dream. They come when they choose. They hate melancholy. They close their fans and throw them on the floor when the music is melancholy. Music comes from the chest. In my chest, they play Spanish madrigals. They hate flamenco. I'll change my tune. What can I sing? What dance can I hop to? I fail to entertain them. A woman fails to give what is beautiful. I lost my sense of humor. I lost it when I got there and it was snowing. In spring, it snowed. White flakes came down off the rooftop and glided down to the suitcases where I stood in my Kletter boots, corduroy pants, and thin jacket. Snow was a wonder then.

Sweet floating wonder. Shave ice in the air, coming down freely, self-willed. It snowed too long. Things went wrong. No one upstairs grinding shave ice in Mo'ili'ili and dumping it into a white cone cup...yellow and cherry ribbons of syrup dribbling down the side. Why do I have my sense of humor here? Its value is not as great, here. Here it is warm, and the trees curve and there are ribs of dinosaurs: coconut tree ribs conquered by the Samoans, lying on the ground. Here it is so beautiful, you can afford to be serious...

UMBRELLAS

Umbrellas are opening up
all over campus for the rain
one

                         here

one

           here

like the sea vegetation
of soft chiffon berets
pink caps with water veins
and green stem umbrella handles

We see green through
the pink translucency
the algae alpha source
the water filled with nutrients
the feeding ground, playground of fish
who breathe in water flow motions
this motion of ballerinas—
white swans on a lake
in the motion we call "classical"

The breathing gill fish swim

alternating between sea strands
through

here
                              through

here
                    through

here

singing songs through their gills
like angels with their xylophones
wax paper comb songs children make
the songs of umbrellas that open for rain

CLARITY

Clarity is in the bell we hear
as in bluebell
or the trueness of color
as in marigold
though the trueness of what it repels
is arguable.
The flowers we are
or the flowers we choose
or the blossoms of what we wish for the world
seem to be things
no one has time to consider anymore.
Who sits on hilltops now and ink brushes the trees
as the mist rolls over them in dreamy sleep
and who writes syllables
to the moon
with flourishes
or draws a cricket playing a fiddle
while a spider may weave its web
on a loom?
Who'll be the one
to peek out the window
to see what glows like a firefly
with gauzy wings shaped
like a plump translucent
cherub?
Someone will raise a hand
or won't raise a hand
but will pause one night
at the window.

NECKLACE, PLEASE

String me together a necklace, please!
Please find me periwinkle shells—
they're lavender.

Lavender is an introduction to the sea.
It tells you not to expect anything you've ever seen before.
It says let go of the bundle of thatch in your fist.

It says make an arc with your arms
and swim through the days
like a crab going sideways—
down the boardwalk
the hard way.
Make two circles with your arms.
Peer in.
You've made the submarine hatch
to visit creatures who have phosphorous hair
and as decoration
they sometimes attach rubies to their teeth.

Hear—
it is a circus.
Circuits turned on by sea lights.
Sea cabbages roll.

They are overweight angelfish
tangled up in their own chiffon tail vanity.
Clams collect on the bottom
and one pearl busies itself
smoothening its side

glowing blue
loving luster
sending out lavender hues.

THE DINOSAUR CLUB

There are rough energies
out there in that world
and it's something that I don't understand.

What happened to the ever-prevailing water
that used to smooth out these fellows?
"They used it covering dinosaurs."
Green dinosaurs walking
so large that lichen grew on their feet
thinking they were rocks.

But captured in rock were also shells or sea bits or ferns
with not-yet -exposed spores.
Dazzling a woman
are gold spurs and spores.
Dazzled,
she couldn't bear the indelicacy
of the large club of a dinosaur—
club club
walking on earth.

These energies are still walking around
in the land of this year.
Walking, they seep out of corners
or bump into your shoulder.

To soothe them,
women come as rain
washing their skirts in the river.
They wring love and slap cloth
on the rocks
soothing them
smoothening them
making oh so gentle men.

LAYERS

Layer upon layer of creation,
what do we see?
So little.
But we feel tender impulses rising up:
soft songs, barely heard,
ancient songs from underground,
marriages, associations, friendships,
battles.

All written down somewhere on tablets
or marked on cave walls
with roots that made ink.

Streams of people
and the ink on this wall
last through time
to filter up
where people walk
on concrete earth.

On earth
the dirt is packed hard.
Seashells have been crushed
by seas that have long since dried
and that rose to the sky
to feed the the plants that grow.

Sometimes I stand still
and feel all this.
I can't shake it off.

I can only feel
how tender this water is
how tender these impulses
how tenderly they unfold
how difficult it is
to shake off dreams.

DRY-WOOD AND FRAIL-SKIN FAIRIES

Here in the heart of the stump
dry-wood fairies
pour out by the dozens
with shiny red-handle hammers
to build summer cottages
to house
the frail-skin blue fairies
who need houses only at night.
They need to keep their skin damp
so they dip in pools
then run to the houses and write.

Oh yes they write.
This is the fairy that writes.

Fresh out of water
they leave footprints
on the floor.
They shake out their wings
like beach towels and
look sheepish
about the puddles of water around them.

But when they write
they write all night,

candles burning
with their pens making
the scent of red leaves in fall.
And as the papers pile up
they nod their heads to sleep
and lie on cool ti leaves
only to wake in the morning
to the sound of shiny hammers.

Dipping into pools
they run again
to find the new bright houses
the dry-wood fairies make.

THE GROVE
Excerpt from *Old Volcano Road*, a novella

Eva is relying on the help of Null to save the life of her brother, Gene. On their journey, Null takes her to an unexpected place.

Drowsy, she settled beneath another tree. They seemed to wait forever. Null didn't seem impatient, but he was hard to read. She started to say something but calmed herself by looking upward.

After an hour or so, Null got up and listened as if he heard something. Eva stood up, and Null gave her a look. "Take your cues from me and them," he repeated, and then he led her into the grove.

Eva was directly behind him, and when he finally stopped, she stepped to his right so that she could see for herself what was ahead.

Rise to the window, "Spring, dear!"
Raise up the curtain now
Breathe in the morning glory
Hear all the birds in song

She heard the singing first. Then she saw over a dozen miniature cottages as small as toys, in clusters of four, but not in straight rows. Each cottage had a door or window facing east. It was a small clearing, and she saw very tiny beings, very fuzzy, golden, and gauzy in outline. It was a village, and all the beings were at work.

Sing to the rays of sunshine
Dance to the morning dew
Bow to the scent of flowers
All for the love of you

Some had wings that she could see, and some did not. But the music and voices were what she could hear. She also heard a soft whirring sometimes. As they chopped wood, harvested food, repaired their cottages and tended to plants in the ground, she could hear them.

All joy all joy
Ring true through stone
All joy all joy
Let waters flow

All love, all love
Sing anthems high
All love, all love
For spring is here

She turned to Null, and he smiled. "Be careful," he said again. "They are my friends." Null turned toward them, saying, "They warrant the kindest care."

She heard the tenderness in his voice and realized that it was she who needed to show care with them, and it was their vulnerability, not hers, that he had been alerting her to. Embarrassed, she regretted being cross.

Null stepped forward, and she followed. Eva stepped much more delicately among them, and she saw much they were affected by her thought and mood. Like jellyfish swaying in water, the light beings would fly closer or farther away depending on the nature of her thoughts. Eva gave a quiet smile to Null; he knew she now understood.

The two moved, with the light beings clustering around them, onto a shaded patch of grass. The air hummed, thick with light, and the songs continued. They gathered, creating shining clouds around them, bringing sweets, pitchers of water, fruit, and flowers that they pulled in small carts. The sunlight shined through the glass pitchers and everything glowed like honey. Rays also refracted off the Eva's silver cuff, and she thought of the shiny eyes of the woman at the gallery. Null sat closely to her. They were surrounded by gifts and the light beings. He nodded before them, saying very softly, "dear friends."

Come all ye lovers spring's here
All that a heart employs
Move to the spirit growing
Turn to the earth now poised

Strike up the pose of heroes
Take up a gleeful vow
Promise to love unending
Winter is gone for now

They sang as Eva and Null sat among them. Sometimes
the beings flew, and Eva watched them as they circled. They
glowed and the hazy gauze took on different shades of color
and there was so much fragrance in the air. They brought
water bowls and towels so that Null and Eva could wash
their hands and cleanse their faces before eating.

All joy, all joy
Ring true through stone
All joy, all joy
Let waters flow

Eva bowed her head. A deep sweetness rose in her chest.
She looked at Null.

All love, all love
Sing anthems high
All love, all love
For spring is here

The two sat, flooded with attention.

Null closed his eyes.

When he had first begun his missions, Null had so much to learn. He had always had a fiery temperament and impatience with time. His will and moods made him feel so rough and tumble compared to others who did this work.

After an early mission, he had been sent to this grove to meet with the small light beings, all just two to three inches in size. He didn't know why he was sent to them. They had just begun work to develop the grove. He guessed he was there to give suggestions on their work. There were only three completed cottages, and they had the beginnings of the vegetable plots and gardens. He was first introduced to Cable, who, at three inches, was one of the tallest in height and the primary handler for their projects. Though translucent, Cable had the form of a stocky craftsman with a tool belt, and he showed Null around the grove and their projects. Null felt clumsy, kneeling down to look at the tiny but developing home structures, lanes, and water wells. He often didn't know what to say, other than "good" or "I see." At the same time, their industriousness impressed him.

Cable didn't seem to mind Null's lack of conversation, and after the tours of the latest improvements, Null would sit with Cable and the small beings and they would feast. Music, singing, colorful light displays would follow for several hours. The celebrating made Null the most uncomfortable. He didn't have much to say and often spent time wondering about the next mission, but he was polite to his hosts. Though he still didn't know what to make of what they did, he was courteous and expressed his appreciation.

In an early visit, after a particularly hard mission, Null had come to the grove. What he had done had been successful, but only after a long battle. Null walked up the grove but Cable, who had initially flown happily toward him, drew back, and the small beings all clustered behind Cable. Edgy and irked, Null had been required to come. Cable and the beings' spirits dropped. Something pulled in Null's heart, and a sway of anger, sorrow, and fear moved through him. He struggled against it at first, but then realized he was exhausted. Cable drew nearer to help, and as Null lay upon the soft summer grass, Cable and the other small light beings began to hover over him, forming a thick blanket of light. As they did, light began to seep into Null's chest. They stayed hovering for several hours. Knots throughout his body began to untie. He realized he was being reworked, and the reworking was for peace. At one point he opened his eyes, and he saw Cable, whose eyes were closed, hovering above him. Ashamed of how he had treated Cable before, he knew how little of himself he had revealed, and now he felt so small next to them.

After several hours, the light beings gradually flew back to their work. Null had sat up slowly, and Cable led him to the river. Null pulled the clothing off of his tired limbs and slid his body into the water. He moved his palm across his chest. It was as if his heart and ribs were resettling, and what had covered his soul had broken apart and then come together again in waves. He lay in the river feeling warm, then cold, then hot, then cool. Cable stayed on the banks throughout. There were moments Null opened his eyes to glance at Cable, and Cable would nod, and Null would continue. They remained that way until night.

When Null pulled himself out of the river, Cable had blanket and dry clothes waiting for him. "You won't see me again, that way. I mean, so rough," Null said, as the two sat by the river. As they two sat, looking at the moving water, and the sun slipping away, Null turned to him and said, "You are a friend."

Cable nodded, a tear sliding down his face, which he didn't wipe away, saying, "We are always here for you, Null, and you are here for us." They sat together without speaking until deep into the night, returning to the grove for a celebration around the fire. The small beings were clustered in small rings. They made up songs to sing at that moment, and there were platters of food they had roasted from the crops they had grown in the gardens.

So now, as he sat next to Eva, he knew she would have questions of why they were here. But whatever questions she had, the gifts the beings gave were soaking into them, and he knew that she needed them, whether she knew it or not.

Eva and Null sat together with eyes closed, and when Null opened his eyes again, he looked toward Cable, who met his glance. Whatever lay ahead, they were now blessed and honored.

Allow me to praise the forest
Allow me to praise the sky

Allow me to praise the echo
Of unbounded endless joy
Unbounded endless joy

They spent the day feasting, eating, lying in the grass, looking up at the sky, enjoying the beauty of the small beings. Occasionally Eva would look at Null. He knew she was thinking of time, but she had remembered to take her cues from him. She thought of Gene, but she also sensed peace here, and when she did, she sent this feeling to Gene. He would be flooded with this as much as she was. Wherever he was, and whatever he was feeling, he would feel this too.

As Eva sat in the grove, Cable came up to her and said, "This is our way. We work and we celebrate." She looked at his impish face and the hammer hung on a loop on a workman's belt around his waist. He was translucent and the light he and the other beings had reminded her of hovering fireflies.

As it grew late, Cable and the other beings drew away to their cottages, and at the very edge of the grove, a narrow space remained for Null and Eva to lay down blankets to sleep. Eva looked at the stars. It reminded her of the days when she grew up with Gene. Null seemed to fall straight to sleep. The previous night she had been forty feet up, and tonight she was on the forest floor, but she was still floating, as if she were above the trees. She let herself think about nothing but the stream of joy that ran through her. Waves of contentment rippled over her body and Null's, and she hoped, over Gene's. They were surrounded by friends. It was as if she were floating up into the sky, barely tethered to the earth, and she fell asleep with that feeling, sliding easily into dreams and into waves that nourished her through the night.

ACKNOWLEDGMENTS

Thank you to family and friends for always supporting me and my writing. Much gratitude to Kumu Kapena and Kumu Lokelani for their encouragement and friendship and for always lifting me up. And lastly, much appreciation to all of the great light beings, large and small, for their love, joy, and presence.

AUTHOR'S NOTE

Some of the most lasting works of fiction, poetry, or art are inexplicably magical yet real. The artists who create them give us experiences that we can't quite explain or reconcile with the everyday world. What I love about artistic minds and souls is the openness to experience and sense of gratitude for it. Through artists, we are allowed into worlds that we wouldn't normally get to see or feel. I'm hoping some of these pieces convey a sense of that.

Some of these pieces are as mysterious to me as they are to everyone else. I just know that when I wrote them, I felt as if they were from a new and different place. I hope that some might also feel familar—that they bring back a sense of elation and wonder—things we felt as children or young adults or at extraordinary moments in our lives. I get those feelings when I read *The Secret Garden* or when I hear people recite lines from *Alice in Wonderland* by heart because they love the book so much.

Even though we are adults, we still have the same spirit we had when we entered the world. In that sense, it's possible that we could have the best of both worlds: our initial spirit but also our adult selves that can drive cars and run away if we have to! And in these times, if anything, we need more moments that are light and celestial. I hope readers will find their own ways to capture any moments they may have like these.

ABOUT THE AUTHOR

Pianta is a writer and editor whose work has appeared in journals such as *Adirondack Review, Nimrod International Journal, Ekphrasis, Terrain.org*, and *Bamboo Ridge Press*. Born and raised on O'ahu, she wrote and taught in California but now lives on the Big Island of Hawai'i. Her readings often incorporate live music, dance, and multimedia. Her projects include a children's CD *Little Bird: Songs for Children* and a novella, *Old Volcano Road*. Her website can be found at www.pianta.org.

ILLUSTRATION CREDITS

Cover illustration, Gerd Altmann, Pixabay.

PUBLICATION CREDITS

"The Grove," excerpted from *Old Volcano Road*, Pianta, 2020; Song lyrics, "Spring," *Little Bird: Songs for Children*, Pianta, 2020.

RELEASES

Old Volcano Road
Novella
Ebook and print versions
Available on Kindle and Amazon

Little Bird: Songs for Children
CD of new, acoustic children's songs
Available on iTunes, Spotify, and Apple Music
Listen to samples at
https://pianta.hearnow.com/

Little Bird: Songs for Children Songbook
Accompanying songbook of lyrics and guitar chords
Ebook on Apple Books

Hawai'i Poems: from there to here
Book of new and previously published poems
Ebook on Apple Books
Print version on Amazon

Before
Poetry Chapbook
Ebook available on Apple Books
Print version on Amazon

A Man in Parts
Poetry Chapbook
Print version on Amazon

Acts and Intentions
Poetry Chapbook
Print version on Amazon

Love and Grief in the Time of Ketu
Poetry chapbook

Short Fiction
Floating
Ebook on Apple Books
Print version on Amazon

For more information
www.pianta.org

www.ingramcontent.com/pod-product-compliance
Lightning Source LLC
Chambersburg PA
CBHW060630030426
42337CB00018B/3291